MONKEYS/ LOS MONOS

by JoAnn Early Macken

Reading consultant: Susan Nations, M.Ed., author/literacy coach/consultant

WEEKLY WR READER®
EARLY LEARNING LIBRARY

Please visit our web site at: **www.earlyliteracy.cc**
For a free color catalog describing **Weekly Reader®** Early Learning Library's list
of high-quality books, call 1-877-445-5824 (USA) or 1-800-387-3178 (Canada).
Weekly Reader® Early Learning Library's fax: (414) 336-0164.

Library of Congress Cataloging-in-Publication Data available upon request from publisher.
Fax (414) 336-0157 for the attention of the Publishing Records Department.

ISBN 0-8368-4383-5 (lib. bdg.)
ISBN 0-8368-4388-6 (softcover)

This edition first published in 2005 by
Weekly Reader® Early Learning Library
330 West Olive Street, Suite 100
Milwaukee, WI 53212 USA

Copyright © 2005 by Weekly Reader® Early Learning Library

Art direction: Tammy West
Production: Jessica Morris
Photo research: Diane Laska-Swanke
Graphic design: Katherine A. Goedheer
Translation: Tatiana Acosta and Guillermo Gutiérrez

Photo credits: Cover © Ken Lucas/Visuals Unlimited; title, pp. 7, 17, 21 © William Muñoz; pp. 5, 19
© James P. Rowan; p. 9 © Gerald & Buff Corsi/Visuals Unlimited; p. 11 © Rick & Nora Bowers/Visuals
Unlimited; pp. 13, 15 © Joe McDonald/Visuals Unlimited

Printed in the United States of America

1 2 3 4 5 6 7 8 9 09 08 07 06 05 04

Note to Educators and Parents

Reading is such an exciting adventure for young children! They are beginning to integrate their oral language skills with written language. To encourage children along the path to early literacy, books must be colorful, engaging, and interesting; they should invite the young reader to explore both the print and the pictures.

Animals I See at the Zoo is a new series designed to help children read about twelve fascinating animals. In each book, young readers will learn interesting facts about the featured animal.

Each book is specially designed to support the young reader in the reading process. The familiar topics are appealing to young children and invite them to read — and re-read — again and again. The full-color photographs and enhanced text further support the student during the reading process.

In addition to serving as wonderful picture books in schools, libraries, homes, and other places where children learn to love reading, these books are specifically intended to be read within an instructional guided reading group. This small group setting allows beginning readers to work with a fluent adult model as they make meaning from the text. After children develop fluency with the text and content, the book can be read independently. Children and adults alike will find these books supportive, engaging, and fun!

Una nota a los educadores y a los padres

¡La lectura es una emocionante aventura para los niños! En esta etapa están comenzando a integrar su manejo del lenguaje oral con el lenguaje escrito. Para fomentar la lectura desde una temprana edad, los libros deben ser vistosos, atractivos e interesantes; deben invitar al joven lector a explorar tanto el texto como las ilustraciones.

Animales que veo en el zoológico es una nueva serie pensada para ayudar a los niños a conocer cuatro animales fascinantes. En cada libro, los jóvenes lectores conocerán datos interesantes sobre ellos.

Cada libro ha sido especialmente diseñado para facilitar el proceso de lectura. La familiaridad con los temas tratados atrae la atención de los niños y los invita a leer — y releer — una y otra vez. Las fotografías a todo color y el tipo de letra facilitan aún más al estudiante el proceso de lectura.

Además de servir como fantásticos libros ilustrados en la escuela, la biblioteca, el hogar y otros lugares donde los niños aprenden a amar la lectura, estos libros han sido concebidos específicamente para ser leídos en grupos de instrucción guiada. Este contexto de grupos pequeños permite que los niños que se inician en la lectura trabajen con un adulto cuya fluidez les sirve de modelo para comprender el texto. Una vez que se han familiarizado con el texto y el contenido, los niños pueden leer los libros por su cuenta. ¡Tanto niños como adultos encontrarán que estos libros son útiles, entretenidos y divertidos!

— Susan Nations, M.Ed., author, literacy coach,
and consultant in literacy development

I like to go to the zoo.
I see monkeys at the zoo.

— — — — — — —

Me gusta ir al zoológico.
En el zoológico veo monos.

"Ooh, eek," monkeys whoop and shriek. **It** is fun to watch them play.

- - - - - - - -

Los monos gritan y **chillan**: "uuuu, iiiik". Es divertido verlos jugar.

vines/
lianas

Some monkeys look for food in the trees. They may eat leaves, flowers, insects, or fruit.

＝ ＝ ＝ ＝ ＝ ＝ ＝ ＝

Algunos monos buscan comida en los árboles. Pueden comer hojas, flores, insectos o frutas.

Some monkeys live in the trees. Some monkeys live on the ground.

- - - - - - -

Algunos monos viven en los árboles. Algunos monos viven en el suelo.

Some monkeys are small
and furry.

- - - - - - - -

Algunos monos son
pequeños y peludos.

Some monkeys are large and **fierce**.

- - - - - - -

Algunos monos son grandes y **feroces**.

Me gusta ver los monos en el zoológico. ¿Y a ti?

- - - - - - -

I like to see monkeys at the zoo. Do you?

Glossary/Glosario

fierce — wild, cruel

feroz — salvaje, cruel

shriek — to cry out in a loud piercing way

chillar — gritar haciendo un sonido penetrante y fuerte

vines — plants with long, thin stems

lianas — plantas de tallos largos y delgados

For More Information/Más información

Books/Libros

Arnold, Caroline. *Monkey*. New York: Morrow Junior
    Books, 1993.

Greenwood, Elinor. *Rain Forest*. New York: DK Publishing,
    2001.

Shahan, Sherry. *Feeding Time at the Zoo*. New York:
    Random House, 2000.

Web Sites/Páginas Web

Chaffee Zoo

www.chaffeezoo.org/zoo/animals/colobus.html
For a photo and facts about the colobus monkey
www.chaffeezoo.org/zoo/animals/macaque.html
For a photo and facts about the lion-tailed macaque

exZOOberance.com

www.exzooberance.com/virtual%20zoo/they%20walk/
monkey/monkey.htm
For monkey photos and facts

Index/Índice

About the Author/Información sobre la autora

JoAnn Early Macken is the author of two rhyming picture books, Sing-Along Song and Cats on Judy, and four other series of nonfiction books for beginning readers. Her poems have appeared in several children's magazines. A graduate of the M.F.A. in Writing for Children and Young Adults program at Vermont College, she lives in Wisconsin with her husband and their two sons. Visit her Web site at www.joannmacken.com.

JoAnn Early Macken es autora de dos libros infantiles ilustrados en verso, Sing-Along Song y Cats on Judy, y también de cuatro series de libros de corte realista dirigidos a los lectores principiantes. Sus poemas han sido publicados en varias revistas para niños. Graduada del M.F.A. en Redacción para niños y adultos jóvenes del Vermont College, vive en Wisconsin con su esposo y sus dos hijos. Visita su página Web. www.joannmacken.com.